Ellie Changes Color

by Dawn Riley

This book is dedicated to

Leighton
and her best friend, Ellie

Ickerly

Wickerly

Wooooo

Ellie's the color...

BLUE

Wickity

Wockity

Weeen

Ellie's the color... 

GREEN

Happily

Dapperly

Eddd

Ellie's the color...

RED

Yockity

Dockity

Dellow

Ellie's the color...

YELLOW

slipperty

sloperty

slurple

Ellie's the color...

PURPLE

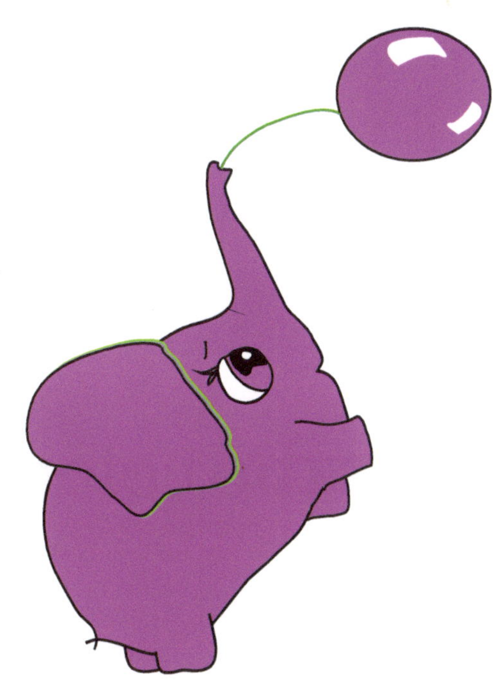

Tinkerly

Winkerly

Light

Ellie's the color...

WHITE

Tipperty

Topity

Tink

Ellie's the color...

PINK

Pickerty
Pockerty
Porrange

Ellie's the color...

ORANGE

Hoppity

Doppity

Dak

Ellie's the color...

BLACK

Ellie is all the colors...

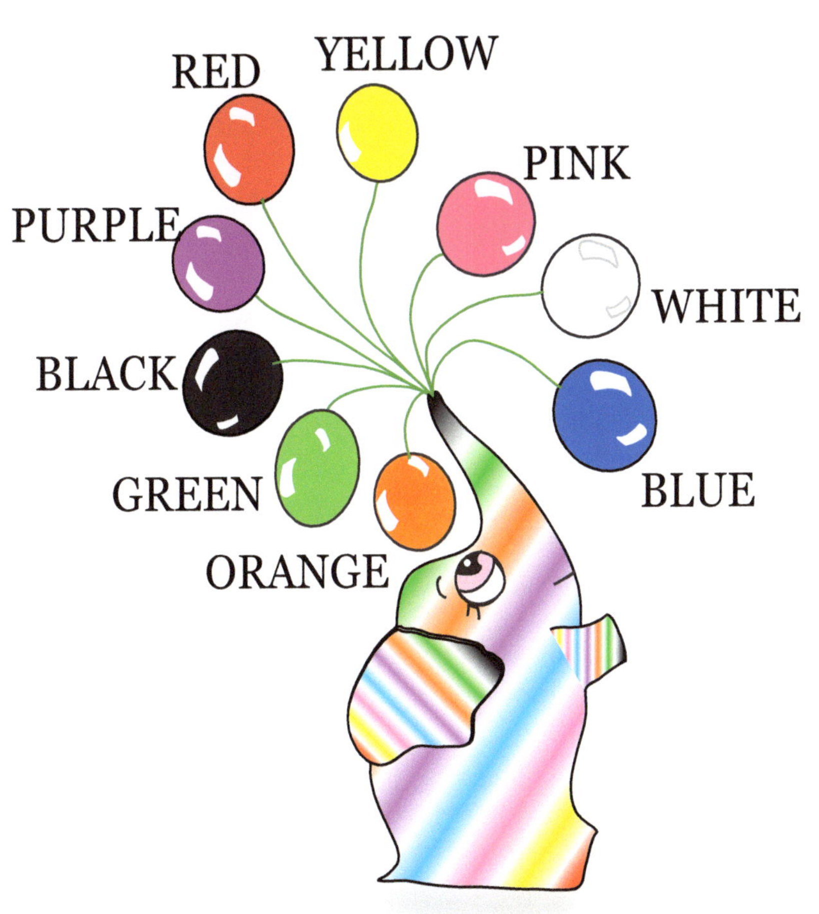
RED
YELLOW
PINK
PURPLE
WHITE
BLACK
BLUE
GREEN
ORANGE

Ellie Changes Color

© Copyright 2016 Dawn Riley

All rights reserved.

Cover design by Dawn Riley
Written and illustrated by Dawn Riley

This book is copyright. Except for the purposes of fair review, no part may be stored or transmitted in any form or by any means, electronic or mechanical, including recording or storage in any information retrieval system, without permission in writing from the publisher. No reproduction may be made, whether by photocopying or by any other means, unless a license has been obtained from the publisher or its agent.

The publishers and author can accept no legal responsibility for any consequences arising from the application of information, advice or instructions given in this publication.

First published 2016 by
Riley Hooper Ltd

Printed in the United States of America

ISBN-13   978-0473379315
ISBN-10   0473379317

www.ingramcontent.com/pod-product-compliance
Lightning Source LLC
Chambersburg PA
CBHW041229050726

47599CB00001B/127